NATIONAL
GEOGRAPHIC

# STAR POWER

**PATHFINDER EDITION**

By Don Thomas and Elizabeth Sengel

CONTENTS

# OUR STAR, THE SUN

By Don Thomas

NASA ASTRONAUT

**Blast off with an astronaut on a journey to the stars.**

# I had been waiting for this moment since I was six years old.

I was lying on my back, strapped inside my seat in the space shuttle *Columbia*. It was minutes before launch and my first trip into space.

Six seconds before liftoff, the three main engines roared to life. My seat bucked, rattled, and rolled. If I hadn't been strapped in, the rumbling would have tossed me to the floor.

*Columbia* blasted skyward. At that moment, I felt like there was a hand on the middle of my back, a hand that was pushing me straight up into the sky. As *Columbia* sped upward, I was yelling inside my helmet, "Yahoo! Let's go!" No one could hear me over the engines.

Eight and a half minutes later, everything went silent as the main engines shut down. Another wave of excitement hit me as I realized I'd made it—I was in space. Now I was eager to get my first view of Earth from space.

## Sunrise, Sunset

I unstrapped myself and floated to a window. Nothing could have prepared me for what I saw. As I pressed my nose to the glass, I gasped. The view took my breath away.

The velvety blackness of the sky jumped out at me. It was darker than any color I had ever seen. The inky darkness seemed like it was glowing black. A bright blue layer of Earth's atmosphere met with the blackness of space.

Before long, I saw the first of many sunsets from the shuttle. Sunset and sunrise are much different in space.

On Earth, we can see one sunrise and one sunset each day, which is caused by Earth's **rotation**, or spinning on its **axis**. It takes 24 hours for Earth to complete one rotation.

The shuttle orbits, or goes around, Earth every 90 minutes, which means I could see 16 sunrises and sunsets each day. During my trip, I could have seen more than a hundred.

**Sinking Sun.** *Earth's atmosphere changes color as the sun sets.*

**Flaming Flares.** *Bright arches of hot, glowing gas erupt from the surface of the sun.*

## Our Starry Neighbor

The space shuttle whips around Earth at 28,000 kilometers (17,500 miles) per hour. At that speed, sunsets seem to happen much faster than they do on Earth, occurring so quickly that you could easily miss one. In only 13 seconds, I saw Earth's atmosphere change from daytime blue to orange to deep red to nighttime black.

From Earth or the shuttle, the sun is the brightest object in the sky. It is also the largest object in our solar system. One million planets the size of Earth could fit inside it.

Yet the sun is just an average-size star. Stars are giant balls of hot gases, which function as a star's fuel. Stars change their fuel into energy. We see and feel some of this energy as heat and light. Most stars have enough fuel to make heat and light for billions of years.

It takes a little more than eight minutes for the sun's light, flowing from the sun and traveling through space, to reach Earth. That means the sunlight you are seeing right now left the sun about eight minutes ago.

## Spots and Flares

With the unaided eye, the sun looks quiet and calm, but you can see something completely different through a **telescope**. Now the sun looks dynamic. Gases boil and pop, and fiery storms rage across its super-hot surface.

One kind of storm, called sunspots, looks like dark blotches. A sunspot looks dark because it is cooler than the areas around it. At times, many sunspots speckle the sun, but at other times, there are few or no spots. The number of spots follows an 11-year cycle. As the cycle moves forward, we are able to see more and more spots.

Solar flares, which form when gases and energy explode from the sun's surface, often materialize around sunspots. The jet of energy from a solar flare shoots into space, reaching Earth in just a few days.

Colliding with Earth's atmosphere, the energy streams toward Earth's poles. It causes gases in the atmosphere to glow green, blue, red, and even pink! We call these shimmering colors auroras.

## Our Solar System

Energy from the sun not only warms Earth, but it also warms all the planets. A planet is a large space object that orbits a star. In all, eight planets orbit our sun. Four of these planets, which are called the inner planets, are small, rocky worlds. The other four, called the outer planets, are gas giants.

Jupiter is the largest of these worlds. It has a ring and more moons than any other planet. It also is almost completely made of gases, which move constantly. Colorful clouds churn around storms, and bolts of lightning streak. The Great Red Spot, the largest storm on any planet in the solar system, whips around. Auroras even shimmer above the planet's poles.

## Star Light, Star Bright

From the space shuttle, I had a grand view of the sun, Earth, and other planets. I also could see many more stars than I could ever see from the ground.

On Earth, the atmosphere blocks some of the light from each star. The atmosphere not only dims starlight, it changes it. Moving gases cause stars to twinkle, but in space, stars don't twinkle. They look like steady points of light.

From the shuttle, I could see stars of different colors—white, blue, red, and even yellow, like our sun. Color **tells** a lot about a star. For example, it can tell you how hot a star is. Cooler stars are red, warm stars are yellow, and the hottest stars are blue.

Since we can see stars more clearly from space, NASA has placed telescopes there. The Hubble Space Telescope is probably the best known space telescope. Launched into space more than 20 years ago, Hubble can see objects 50 times fainter than the most powerful telescope on Earth can see.

So far, Hubble has orbited Earth many times, traveling nearly five billion kilometers (three billion miles). Along the way, it has taken hundreds of thousands of pictures of objects in space.

**Giant Jupiter.**
*Streams of gas swirl around Jupiter, the largest planet in our solar system.*

# A Star Is Born

Some of the most eye-catching pictures from Hubble show nebulae, which are clouds of gas and dust in space. Nebulae form amazing shapes and can have brilliant colors.

Some nebulae are nurseries for stars. The Carina Nebula is one of the best known nurseries. From Earth, it can only be seen from the Southern Hemisphere.

Stars form inside this nebula and others like it. Bits of gas and dust come together. **Gravity** pulls in more and more gas and dust, molding them into a sphere.

The sphere grows larger and larger. Eventually, the sphere's gravity grows so powerful that the sphere collapses into itself. As it collapses, the gases grow hotter and hotter. If the gases reach tens of millions of degrees, a star is born! Of course, this doesn't happen all at once. It takes millions of years for a new star to begin to shine.

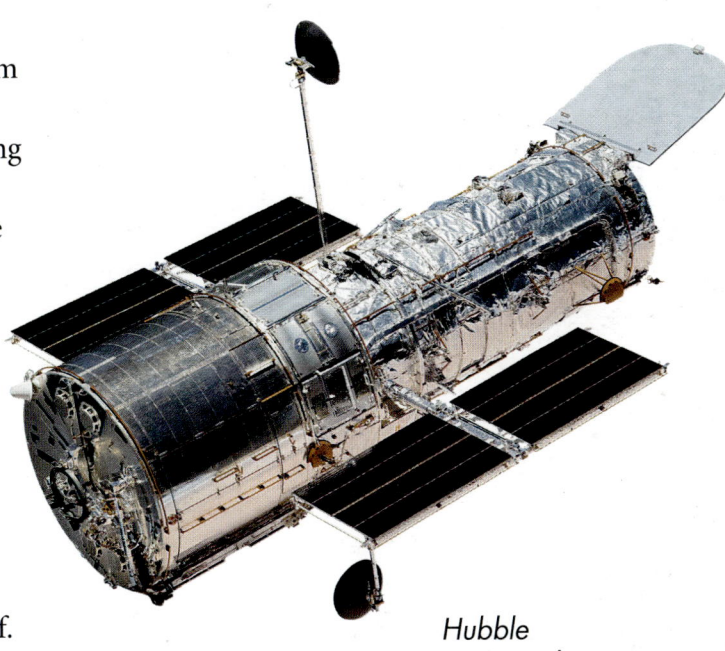

*Hubble Space Telescope*

**Star Babies.** *New stars are being born in the Carina Nebula.*

## Dying Stars

Most stars live for millions or billions of years. How long a star lives depends on how big it is. The largest and hottest stars, which live for only a few million years, have the shortest lives. Smaller stars tend to live longer because they don't use up their fuel as fast. Our sun, which we expect to burn for another five billion years, is about halfway through its life.

A star's size also affects how it dies. When a star the size of our sun runs out of fuel, it puffs out its outer layers of gas and slowly dims. Eventually it becomes a black dwarf—a frozen ball floating through space.

## Galaxies Ahead

A group of millions of stars is called a **galaxy**. In our own galaxy, the Milky Way, the sun is just one of about 100 billlion stars.

Hubble has shown us some spectacular examples of galaxies. Many are spirals like the Milky Way. One is shaped like a tadpole, while another looks like the eye of a cat.

From *Columbia*, the sky looked alive with more stars than I could ever count. A couple of my favorite things to see were the Large and Small Magellanic Clouds, a pair of small galaxies that orbit the Milky Way. A small galaxy has fewer than a billion stars.

**Final Breath.** *The Helix Nebula is a ring of gas around a dying star.*

**Star Burst.** *An exploding giant star formed the Crab Nebula.*

Really big stars collapse on themselves when they run out of fuel. The outermost layer of a large star explodes into space, and the star's outer layers form a kind of nebula around the dying star. The explosion is called a supernova.

The largest stars have mysterious endings. Gravity causes a giant star to collapse on itself. It collapses so fast and violently that it becomes a black hole. Gravity squeezes all the star stuff into a pinpoint. No one knows what happens inside a black hole. We know little about black holes because their gravity is so strong, nothing, not even light, can escape them.

Through a pair of binoculars, I could see these fuzzy patches of light come into focus, but I had to look quickly because my view was about to change. Another spectacular sunrise was on its way. The light and heat felt good on my face as the sunlight streamed through the windows of *Columbia*.

After staring at all the strange and wonderful sights in the night sky, it was good to see the old familiar sun once again. I soon realized that as amazing as stars, nebulae, black holes, and galaxies are, there's no place like home, our planet Earth.

**Starry Spiral.** *Billions of stars make up the Whirlpool galaxy. Its curving spiral arms house young stars, while older stars shine in its yellowish core.*

# WORDWISE

**axis:** line about which a rotating body such as Earth turns

**galaxy:** system of stars

**gravity:** pulling force that all objects have

**rotation:** act of turning around a center

**telescope:** device used to study distant objects

# Powered
## by the Sun

BY ELIZABETH SENGEL

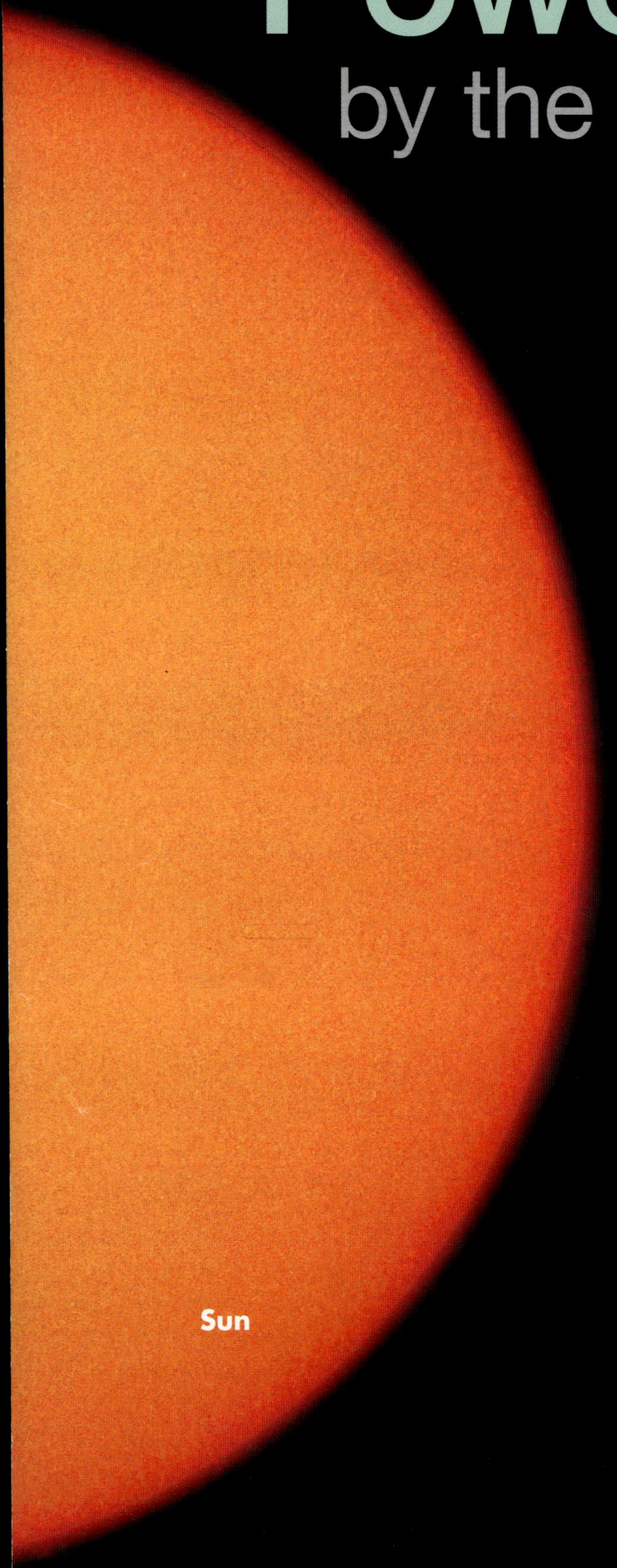

The International Space Station (ISS) is a floating home and laboratory. It glides 386 kilometers (240 miles) above Earth, orbiting the planet every 92 minutes. It contains living facilities for the crew and laboratories for research and experiments. How does this amazing spacecraft get electricity to keep everything running?

The answer is the sun. The ISS is equipped with eight solar arrays, or panels. All together, these immense structures, which look like wings, equal about half the size of a United States football field. They are blanketed with solar cells—262,400 to be exact. A solar cell, or photovoltaic cell, is a tiny device that converts sunshine into electricity.

A computer keeps the solar arrays tilting toward the sun. To power the spacecraft when it's traveling in Earth's shadow, the crew uses batteries. The batteries are recharged every time the ISS is in sunlight.

Sun

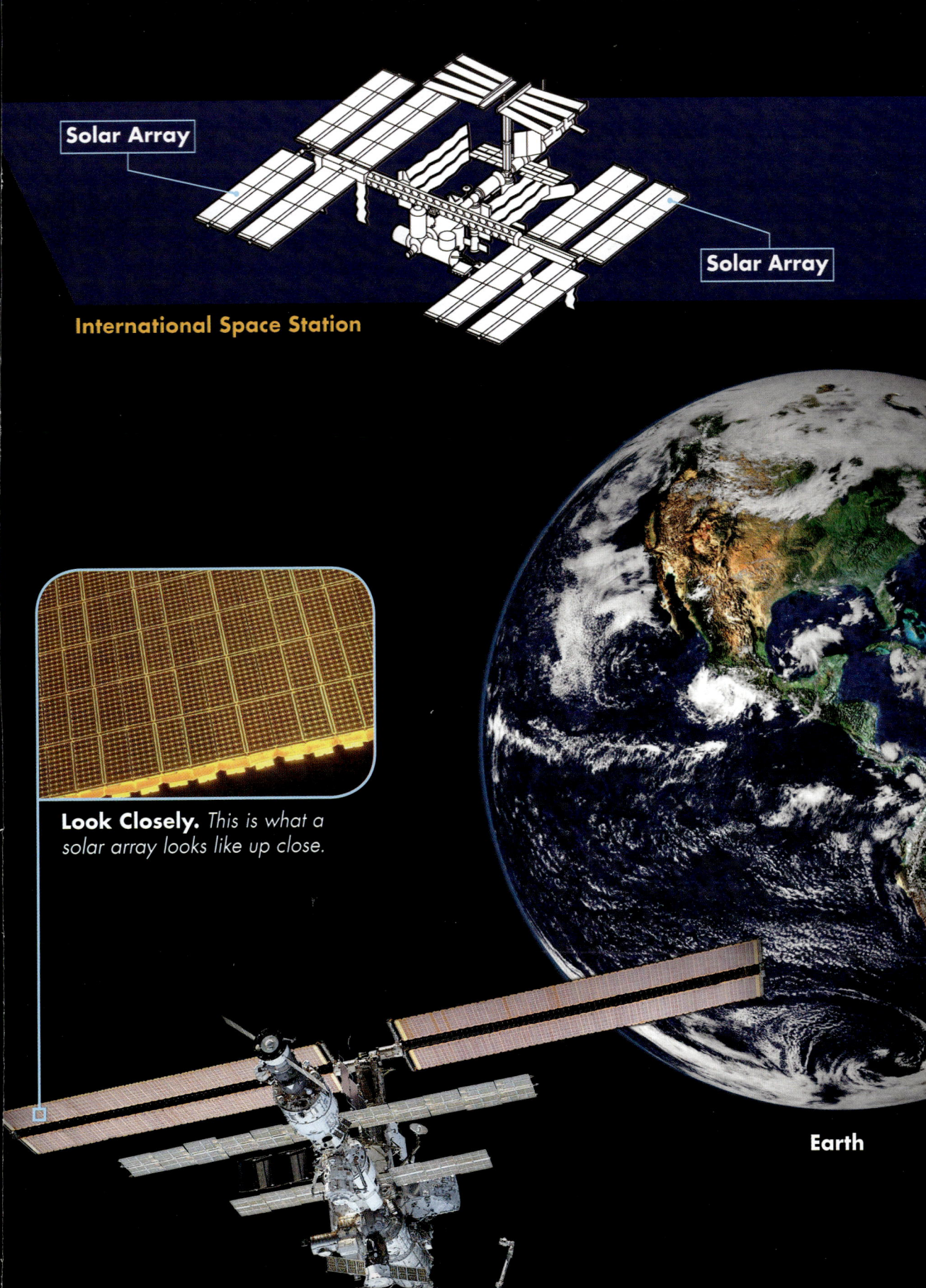

Solar Array

Solar Array

**International Space Station**

**Look Closely.** *This is what a solar array looks like up close.*

Earth

# Shining STAR

**Follow the stars to answer these questions about the sun and its energy.**

1. Where do stars get their energy?

2. How might our sun have formed?

3. How does a star's size affect the way it dies?

4. Why does Don Thomas say there is no place like Earth?

5. Why does the ISS have solar arrays? What do they look like?